KEEP CALM AND RUN ON

KEEP CALM AND RUN ON

KEEP CALM AND RUN ON

KEEP CALM AND RUN ON

KEEP CALM AND RUN ON

KEEP CALM AND RUN ON

KEEP CALM AND RUN ON

KEEP CALM AND RUN ON

KEEP CALM AND RUN ON

KEEP CALM AND RUN ON

KEEP CALM AND RUN ON

KEEP CALM AND RUN ON

KEEP CALM AND RUN ON

KEEP CALM AND RUN ON

Summersdale Publishers Ltd
46 West Street
Chichester
West Sussex
PO19 1RP
UK

www.summersdale.com

Printed and bound in the Czech Republic

ISBN: 978-1-84953-739-1

Substantial discounts on bulk quantities of Summersdale books are available to corporations, professional associations and other organisations. For details contact Nicky Douglas by telephone: +44 (0) 1243 756902, fax: +44 (0) 1243 786300 or email: nicky@summersdale.com.

KEEP
CALM
AND
RUN
ON

summersdale

Perseverance, secret
of all triumphs.

Victor Hugo

You don't have to be great
to start, but you have
to start to be great.

Zig Ziglar

For me… running is the answer. Out on the road it is just you, the pavement, and your will.

John Bingham

Failure will never overtake me if my determination to succeed is strong enough.

Og Mandino

What I've learned from
running is that the time
to push hard is when…
you want to give up.

James Dyson

Run like hell and get
the agony over with.

Clarence DeMar

My feeling is that any day I am too busy to run is a day that I am too busy.

John Bryant

A marathon is like life with
its ups and downs, but
once you've done it, you
feel you can do anything.

Anonymous

The biggest mistake an athlete can make is to be afraid of making one.

L. Ron Hubbard

Ninety-eight per cent
of success is in the
head and the heart.

Cathy Ferguson

The greater danger for
most of us lies not in
setting our aim too high
and falling short; but in
setting our aim too low,
and achieving our mark.

Michelangelo

Racing teaches us to challenge ourselves. It teaches us to push beyond where we thought we could go.

PattiSue Plumer

In running it is man against himself... in his ability, with brain and heart to master himself and his emotions.

Glenn Cunningham

There's no such
thing as bad weather,
just soft people.

Bill Bowerman

If you can train your mind
for running, everything
else will be easy.

Amby Burfoot

Good things come
slow – especially in
distance running.

Bill Dellinger

Desire is the most
important factor
in the success of
any athlete.

Willie Shoemaker

Nothing splendid has
ever been achieved
except by those who dared
believe that something
inside themselves was
superior to circumstance.

Bruce Barton

I had as many
doubts as anyone
else. Standing on
the starting line,
we're all cowards.

Alberto Salazar

Other people may not
have had high expectations
for me, but I had high
expectations for myself.

Shannon Miller

Athletes need to enjoy their training… From enjoyment comes the will to win.

Arthur Lydiard

Your success and
happiness lies in you.

Helen Keller

Everything you need is already inside.

Bill Bowerman

Pain is inevitable.
Suffering is optional.

Haruki Murakami

Every time I fail I
assume I will be a
stronger person for it.

Joan Benoit Samuelson

A dream doesn't become reality through magic; it takes sweat, determination and hard work.

Colin Powell

Even if you're on the right track, you'll get run over if you just sit there.

Will Rogers

You play the way
you practise.

Pop Warner

I eat whatever the guy who beat me in the last race ate.

Alex Ratelle

The impossible is
often the untried.

Jim Goodwin

It hurts up to a point
and then it doesn't
get any worse.

Ann Trason

The will to win means
nothing if you haven't
the will to prepare.

Juma Ikangaa

Spirit… has fifty times the strength and staying power of brawn and muscle.

Anonymous

Life is thickly sown with thorns, and I know no other remedy than to pass quickly through them. The longer we dwell on our misfortunes, the greater is their power to harm us.

Voltaire

It's not about speed
and gold medals.
It's about refusing
to be stopped.

Amby Burfoot

Keep your dream in
front of you. Never let
it go regardless of how
far-fetched it might seem.

Hal Higdon

You cannot propel
yourself forward
by patting yourself
on the back.

Steve Prefontaine

If the hill has its own
name, then it's probably
a pretty tough hill.

Marty Stern

Success is a state
of mind. If you
want success, start
thinking of yourself
as a success.

Joyce Brothers

You don't get to choose
when opportunity is going
to knock, so you better be
prepared for it when it does.

Ted Anderson

Success is to be
measured not so much
by the position that one
has reached in life as
by the obstacles which
he has overcome while
trying to succeed.

Booker T. Washington

Man imposes his own limitations; don't set any.

Anthony Bailey

The nine inches right here;
set it straight and you can
beat anybody in the world.

Sebastian Coe on the brain

All it takes is all you got.

Marc Davis

The ultimate measure of a man is not where he stands in moments of comfort and convenience, but where he stands at times of challenge and controversy.

Martin Luther King Jr

Don't give up on
the impossible
before you try it.

Clarence Munn

Winners never quit,
and quitters never win.

Vince Lombardi

Now bid me run,
And I will strive with
things impossible.

William Shakespeare

Winning isn't everything.
Wanting to is.

Catfish Hunter

Self-trust is the essence of heroism.

Ralph Waldo Emerson

We all need goals.
Life is hard to live
without one.

Tory Baucum

Many of life's failures are people who did not realise how close they were to success when they gave up.

Thomas Edison

It's good for your legs
and your feet. It's also
very good for the ground.
It makes it feel needed.

Charles M. Schulz on jogging

If the furnace
was hot enough,
anything would burn.

John L. Parker Jr

The thought of… having
to explain to myself
why I didn't run that
morning is enough to
get me out the door.

Linda Johnson

I'd rather run a gutsy
race, pushing all the
way and lose, than
run a conservative
race only for a win.

Alberto Salazar

Motivation is a skill. It can
be learned and practised.

Amby Burfoot

Tough times don't last,
but tough people do.

A. C. Green

Obstacles are those
frightening things you
see when you take your
eyes off the goal.

Henry Ford

There's nothing
a man can't do
if the spirit's there.

Franz Stampfl

Life (and running) is not
all about time but about our
experiences along the way.

Jen Rhines

It's what you learn
after you know it
all that counts.

Earl Weaver

When you come to the
end of your rope,
tie a knot and hang on.

Franklin D. Roosevelt

The greatest pleasure in life is doing what people say you cannot do.

Walter Bagehot

Movement is a medicine for creating change in a person's physical, emotional and mental states.

Carol Welch

Start by doing what's necessary; then do what's possible; and suddenly you are doing the impossible.

St Francis of Assisi

Life equals running and
when we stop running
maybe that's how we'll
know life is finally finished.

Patrick Ness

Strength and growth
come only through
continuous effort
and struggle.

Napoleon Hill

Passion is pushing
myself when there
is no one else around
– just me and the road.

Ryan Shay

Independence is
the outstanding
characteristic of
the runner.

Noël Carroll

Running well is a matter
of having the patience to
persevere when we are
tired and not expecting
instant results.

Robert de Castella

I run because it's
my passion, and
not just a sport.

Sasha Azevedo

We are what we
repeatedly do.
Excellence, then, is
not an act, but a habit.

Aristotle

You have to have
confidence in your ability,
and then be tough enough
to follow through.

Rosalynn Carter

Strength does not
come from physical
capacity. It comes from
an indomitable will.

Mahatma Gandhi

Learn to run when
feeling the pain:
then push harder.

William Sigei

We are ALL runners;
some just run faster
than others.

Bart Yasso

Running is real
and relatively simple...
but it ain't easy.

Mark Will-Weber

Don't bother just to be better than your contemporaries or predecessors. Try to be better than yourself.

William Faulkner

The only way to
discover the limits
of the possible is to
go beyond them into
the impossible.

Arthur C. Clarke

It is exercise alone that
supports the spirits, and
keeps the mind in vigour.

Cicero

Recognise your victories.

Joan Benoit Samuelson

In order to succeed,
we must first believe
that we can.

Nikos Kazantzakis

The race does not always
go to the swift, but to the
ones who keep running.

Anonymous

They succeed,
because they
think they can.

Virgil

Ask yourself:
'Can I give more?'
The answer is usually:
'Yes'.

Paul Tergat

Run when you can, walk
if you have to, crawl if you
must; just never give up.

Dean Karnazes

Our greatest glory
is not in never
falling, but in rising
every time we fall.

Confucius

Once you're beat mentally, you might as well not even go to the starting line.

Todd Williams

The measure of who
we are is what we do
with what we have.

Vince Lombardi

One thing about racing
is that it hurts. You
better accept that from
the beginning or you're
not going anywhere.

Bob Kennedy

Second place is not a defeat. It is a stimulation to get better. It makes you even more determined.

Carlos Lopes

Only those who will risk
going too far can possibly
find out how far one can go.

T. S. Eliot

We all can't be heroes, for someone has to sit on the kerb and clap as they go by.

Will Rogers

Keep your dreams alive.
Understand to achieve
anything requires faith and
belief in yourself, vision,
hard work, determination,
and dedication.

Gail Devers

Don't be pushed by
your problems;
be led by your dreams.

Anonymous

When I do the best
I can with what I
have, then I have
won my race.

Jay Foonberg

Racing is pain,
and that's why you do it,
to challenge yourself and
the limits of your physical
and mental barriers.

Mark Allen

The greatest barrier
to success is the
fear of failure.

Sven-Göran Eriksson

You gain strength,
courage and confidence
by every experience in
which you really stop to
look fear in the face.

Eleanor Roosevelt

You can't win them all – but you can try.

Babe Didrikson Zaharias

The woods are lovely,
dark, and deep,
But I have promises to keep,
And miles to go
before I sleep,
And miles to go
before I sleep.

Robert Frost

If you don't have
confidence, you'll
always find a way
not to win.

Carl Lewis

Joy lies in the fight,
in the attempt, in the
suffering involved, not
in the victory itself.

Mahatma Gandhi

Exercise should be
regarded as tribute
to the heart.

Gene Tunney

Victory is always possible
for the person who
refuses to stop fighting.

Napoleon Hill

Any idiot can train
himself into the
ground; the trick is
working in training to
get gradually stronger.

Keith Brantly

Every defeat, every
heartbreak, every
loss contains its own
seed, its own lesson
on how to improve.

Og Mandino

If what you did yesterday
still looks big to you,
you haven't done much today.

Wid Matthews

By failing to
prepare, you are
preparing to fail.

Benjamin Franklin

The dictionary is the only
place where you come
to SUCCESS before
you get to WORK.

Stubby Currence

Accept the challenges
so that you may
feel the exhilaration
of victory.

George S. Patton

Besides pride,
loyalty, discipline,
heart and mind,
confidence is the
key to all the locks.

Joe Paterno

Most runners run not
because they want to live
longer, but because they
want to live life to the fullest.

Haruki Murakami

Success isn't a result
of spontaneous
combustion. You must
set yourself on fire.

Arnold H. Glasow

I run best when
I run free.

Steve Prefontaine

Running cleared the day's
cobwebs from my mind
and focused my thinking.

Jeff Horowitz

There is something
magical about
running.

Kristin Armstrong

I simply love to run. It's almost like the faster I go, the easier it becomes.

Mary Decker Slaney

Vision without action
is a daydream.

Japanese proverb

Movement is the
essence of life.

Bernd Heinrich

There's only one sensible place for a person to be at 5.30 in the morning. That's in bed… I'm out running.

Derek Clayton

Feel the fear and
do it anyway.

Susan Jeffers

Ability is what you're
capable of doing. Motivation
determines what you do.
Attitude determines
how well you do it.

Lou Holtz

My mindset is: if I'm not out there training, someone else is.

Lynn Jennings

The best thing
about running is the
joy it brings to life.

Kara Goucher

Success doesn't come to you… you go to it.

Marva Collins

Running is one of the best
solutions to a clear mind.

Sasha Azevedo

In order to make dreams
come into reality,
it takes an awful lot of
determination, dedication,
self-discipline and effort.

Jesse Owens

If you want to become
the best runner you
can be, start now.

Priscilla Welch

If you have a bad run, don't obsess about it. You're always going to have days when your legs feel dead.

Heather Hanscom

Get out there and do what you love!

Kara Goucher

When you run in places you
visit, you encounter things
you'd never see otherwise.

Tom Brokaw

Running changed
my life as it will
change yours,
just give it a chance.

Wilfredo Melendez

This is what really
matters: running.
This is where I
know where I am.

Steve Jones

The competition is against
the little voice inside you
that wants to quit.

George Sheehan

The most important
message I stress to
beginners is to learn
to love the sport.

Cliff Held

A runner must run with
dreams in his heart.

Emil Zátopek

Winning doesn't always
mean getting first place;
it means getting the
best out of yourself.

Meb Keflezighi

Life is complicated.
Running is simple.
Is it any wonder that
people like to run?

Kevin Nelson

Running is all about
having the desire to
train and persevere.

Paul Maurer

Run hard,
be strong,
think big!

Percy Cerutty

To win without risk is to triumph without glory.

Pierre Corneille

Every run is a work
of art, a drawing on
each day's canvas.

Dagny Scott Barrios

I often lose motivation,
but it's something I
accept as normal.

Bill Rodgers

There is something about
the ritual of the race...
that brings out the best in us.

Grete Waitz

Stadiums are for spectators.
We runners have nature,
and that is much better.

Juha Väätäinen

The most important
day in any running
programme is rest.

Hal Higdon

Do a little more each
day than you think
you possibly can.

Lowell Thomas

Perseverance is not a long race; it is many short races one after the other.

Walter Elliot

The miracle isn't that I finished. The miracle is that I had the courage to start.

John Bingham

Don't dream of winning. Train for it!

Mo Farah

The five S's of sports
training are: stamina,
speed, strength, skill, and
spirit; but the greatest
of these is spirit.

Ken Doherty

There is no time
to think about how
much I hurt; there
is only time to run.

Ben Logsdon

The reason we race isn't so much to beat each other... but to be with each other.

Christopher McDougall

Never give in, never give in, never, never, never, never.

Winston Churchill

If you're interested in finding out more about our books, find us on Facebook at **Summersdale Publishers** and follow us on Twitter at **@Summersdale**

www.summersdale.com